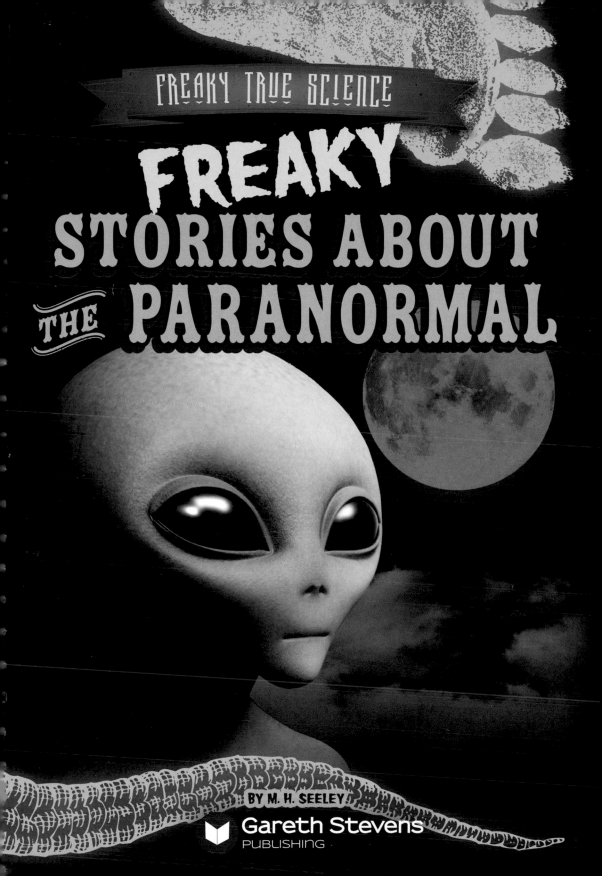

FREAKY TRUE SCIENCE

FREAKY
STORIES ABOUT
THE PARANORMAL

BY M. H. SEELEY

Gareth Stevens
PUBLISHING

rease visit our website, www.garethstevens.com. For a free color catalog of
all our high-quality books, call toll free 1-800-542-2595 or fax 1-877-542-2596.

Library of Congress Cataloging-in-Publication Data

Names: Seeley, M. H., author.
Title: Freaky stories about the paranormal / M.H. Seeley.
Description: New York : Gareth Stevens Publishing, 2016. | Series: Freaky
  true science | Includes index.
Identifiers: LCCN 2015050132 | ISBN 9781482448467 (pbk.) | ISBN 9781482448498
  (library bound) | ISBN 9781482448474 (6 pack)
Subjects: LCSH: Parapsychology–Juvenile literature. | Curiosities and
  wonders–Juvenile literature.
Classification: LCC BF1031 .S425 2016 | DDC 130–dc23
LC record available at https://lccn.loc.gov/2015050132

First Edition

Published in 2017 by
Gareth Stevens Publishing
 11 East 14th Street, Suite 349
New York, NY 10003

Designer: Sarah Liddell
Editor: Ryan Nagelhout

Photo credits: Cover, p. 1 (alien) Albert Ziganshin/Shutterstock.com; cover, p. 1 (foot)
Anna Rassadnikova/Shutterstock.com; cover, p. 1 (tail used throughout book) IADA/
Shutterstock.com; cover, p. 1 (background used throughout book) Shukaylova Zinaida/
Shutterstock.com; pp. 5, 7, 9, 11, 13, 15, 17, 19, 21, 23, 25, 27, 29 (hand used throughout)
Helena Ohman/Shutterstock.com; pp. 5, 7, 9, 11, 13, 15, 17, 19, 21, 23, 25, 27, 29 (texture
throughout) Alex Gontar/Shutterstock.com; p. 5 (mystery stone) Faolin42/Wikimedia
Commons; p. 5 (Antikythera Mechanism) LOUISA GOULIAMAKI/Stringer/AFP/Getty
Images; p. 5 (Dorchester pot) BCtl/Wikimedia Commons; p. 5 (Newark Holy Stones)
Goneln60/Wikimedia Commons; p. 7 Durova/Wikimedia Commons; p. 9 Eric Raptosh
Photography/Blend Images/Getty Images; pp. 11, 12 Scewing/Wikimedia Commons;
p. 13 (main) Ctac/Wikimedia Commons; p. 13 (inset) Svajcr/Wikimedia Commons;
p. 15 Time & Life Pictures/Contributor/The LIFE Picture Collection/Getty Images;
p. 16 ellepistock/Shutterstock.com; p. 17 VICTOR HABBICK VISIONS/Science Photo
Library/Getty Images; p. 19 PASIEKA/Science Photo Library/Getty Images;
p. 20 Colormos/The Images Bank/Getty Images; p. 21 Universal History Archive/
Contributor/Universal Images Group/Getty Images; p. 23 photo courtesy of NASA;
p. 25 (main) John B. Carnett/Contributor/Popular Science/Getty Images; p. 25 (inset)
Bach01~commonswiki/Wikimedia Commons; p. 27 Mefusbren69/Wikimedia Commons;
p. 29 The Washington Post/Contributor/The Washington Post/Getty Images.

Printed in the United States of America

CPSIA compliance information: Batch #CS16GS: For further information contact Gareth Stevens, New York, New York at 1-800-542-2595

CONTENTS

Words in the glossary appear in **bold** type
the first time they are used in the text.

OUT-OF-PLACE ARTIFACTS

Have you ever opened a drawer in your house and found something that really doesn't belong there, like a spoon in your sock drawer? When it happens in your house, it's just weird. When it happens on an **archaeological** dig, it could be paranormal! "Paranormal" describes anything that can't be readily explained by science. An out-of-place **artifact** (OOPArt) is an object found somewhere (or some time!) it shouldn't be. Sometimes it's "out of place" because its creation requires tools and knowledge that didn't exist. Other OOPArts feature images of people, things, or animals that weren't around yet!

In this book, you'll learn about all kinds of freaky **phenomena**. Some people blame aliens, ghosts, magic, or secret government groups. Others think there's a scientific explanation, we just have to find it!

FREAKY FACTS!

The Antikythera (an-tih-kih-THEER-uh) mechanism, found in a Greek shipwreck in 1900, has been called by some the first mechanical computer and could be more than 2,000 years old!

4

OOPARTS AROUND THE WORLD

SOME SCIENTISTS THINK THEY KNOW WHAT THE ANTIKYTHERA MECHANISM WAS USED FOR, BUT OTHER OOPARTS ARE STILL A MYSTERY!

MYSTERY STONE
A STONE SPHERE COVERED IN MYSTERIOUS SYMBOLS DISCOVERED IN NEW HAMPSHIRE IN 1872.

DORCHESTER POT
A METAL VASE CLAIMED TO HAVE BEEN BLASTED OUT OF SOLID ROCK IN 1852.

NEWARK HOLY STONES
SMALL STONES WITH HEBREW WRITING FOUND IN 1860 ON HOPEWELL NATIVE AMERICAN BURIAL GROUNDS.

ANTIKYTHERA MECHANISM
MYSTERY DEVICE FOUND IN AN ANCIENT GREEK SHIPWRECK.

SCIENCE OR SUPERNATURAL?

One person's fact is someone else's fiction when the paranormal is involved. Most scientists think OOPArts are **pseudoscience**, wishful thinking, scientific misunderstanding, or stem from a lack of understanding about the culture the object belongs to. In some cases, scientists have suggested that some OOPArts are hoaxes, which are pranks or tricks. One OOPArt turned out to just be a 1920s spark plug! But others can't be explained quite so easily and remain a mystery.

THE PIED PIPER OF HAMELIN

We've all heard the fairy tale: a **medieval** town with a rat problem hires a musician to lure the rats away with his music. After he does, the townspeople refuse to pay him, and as punishment, he plays a song that lures all the town's children away, never to be seen again. Freaky, right?

Well, that's probably what the townspeople of Hamelin said when it happened to them sometime around the year 1300. According to a story shown on a stained-glass window in the local church, a group of 130 children from the town were simply "lost" and never seen again. Accounts tell of a man dressed in many colors and playing a flute who led the children away. Where did they go, and why? We may never know the answer.

FREAKY FACTS!

In the last place the children were seen, Bungelosenstrasse ("drumless street"), no one is allowed to play music out of respect for the lost children.

RECORDS SAID THAT 130 CHILDREN HAD BEEN "TAKEN FROM THE TOWN BY A PIPER DRESSED IN MANY COLORS."

MEDIEVAL CAREER DAY

There were all kinds of odd jobs in medieval times. A piper's duty was to wake townspeople up in the morning by playing loud music outside their houses, announce special visitors, and provide music during parades. Some jobs, like ewerers, whose only job was to heat up water, aren't around anymore. Other positions still exist, but have changed a lot—for example, barbers back then didn't just cut hair. They were also dentists and even surgeons!

THE TAOS HUM

Only about 2 percent of people can hear it, but for them, the Hum is freaky enough to make them lose their mind—literally. Most people say the mysterious sound is a low rumble that's coming from far away. There are a few "hotspots" where lots of people report being able to hear the Hum. Taos, New Mexico, is one of them, along with Windsor, Ontario; Bristol, England; and Largs, Scotland.

If you're one of the few who can hear the Hum, there's not a lot you can do to avoid it: it's **audible** indoors, outdoors, and even through earplugs. People who can hear the Hum are often called "superhearers" or "hummers" and have complained of headaches, **insomnia**, dizziness, sickness, and even nosebleeds.

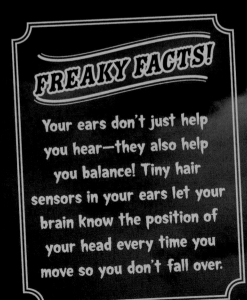

FREAKY FACTS!

Your ears don't just help you hear—they also help you balance! Tiny hair sensors in your ears let your brain know the position of your head every time you move so you don't fall over.

TURN DOWN YOUR MUSIC!

Remember all those times someone told you to turn down the music in your headphones? There's a good reason for it. Really loud noises, including loud music in your headphones, can make you lose your hearing. Some researchers think the Hum may be tinnitus, which is a constant ringing in the ears that can be caused by hearing loss.

FOR PEOPLE WHO ARE ABLE TO HEAR THE HUM, THEY HEAR IT EVERYWHERE, ALL THE TIME.

LINCOLN'S DOPPELGÄNGER

Someone's doppelganger is their exact double—like a paranormal twin. There have been a few famous doppelgänger sightings, but probably one of the freakiest happened to a president of the United States. Abraham Lincoln claimed to have once seen a ghostly double of his own face in the mirror. When he told his wife about it, she predicted that the eerie double was a sign that he would be elected to a second term, and it was so pale because he would "not see life through the last term." In other words, he was sure to be reelected, but at a hefty price.

Anyone with a little knowledge of US presidential history knows this paranormal prediction came exactly true—Lincoln *was* reelected, and he was **assassinated** before the end of his second term.

FREAKY FACTS!

In Norse folklore, doppelgängers were called vardøgers and weren't considered dangerous or evil. Instead, they were thought to be a spirit or guardian that allowed humans to be two places at once.

ABRAHAM LINCOLN

DANGEROUS DOUBLES

Doppelgängers are said to be harbingers of death. A harbinger
is a person or thing that announces the appearance of another.
Some people think that seeing your doppelgänger means you're going
to die soon. English poet Percy Bysshe Shelley saw his doppelgänger
in Italy, pointing toward the Mediterranean Sea, shortly before he
drowned in a boating accident. Queen Elizabeth I of England claimed
to see her doppelgänger asleep in her bed, and not long after, she
died in her sleep.

A doppelgänger isn't the only paranormal thing about the United States' 16th president. He once reported having dreamed of coming upon a group of mourners in the White House. When he asked whom they were mourning, they told him that it was the president, who had been killed by an assassin. He had other dreams like this leading up to his death. The night he was shot, Lincoln told his bodyguard "goodbye" instead of "goodnight."

For many years, people have sighted Lincoln's ghost wandering around the White House. Queen Wilhelmina of the Netherlands said the ghost knocked politely on her door and frightened her so badly she fainted. British Prime Minister Winston Churchill claimed he ran into Lincoln's ghost while getting out of the bath!

FREAKY FACTS!

Two US presidents have died in the White House: William Henry Harrison in 1841 and Zachary Taylor in 1850.

MUMLER'S PHOTO OF MARY TODD LINCOLN AND LINCOLN'S GHOST

FAKE PHOTOGRAPH CREATED BY MUMLER

PRESIDENTIAL AND PARANORMAL

If Lincoln *is* haunting the White House, he certainly isn't lonely. Visitors have claimed to see the ghost of First Lady Abigail Adams wandering around. President Andrew Jackson has also been spotted, and his old bedroom is said to be the most haunted room in the White House. In fact, President Harry Truman wrote that, while he worked, he was often "listening to the ghosts walk up and down the hallway and even right in here in the study."

13

DISAPPEARANCE OF FLIGHT 19

There is a good reason why the Bermuda Triangle is also called the "Devil's Triangle." The region covers a triangle-shaped area in the Atlantic Ocean between Miami, Florida, and the islands of Bermuda and Puerto Rico. It's the last known site of many ships and planes that have mysteriously gone missing.

Five US Navy planes, known collectively as Flight 19, completely vanished on December 5, 1945, after their flight commander sent a message that said, "The ocean doesn't look as it should." Their compasses couldn't find north. High winds came out of nowhere. The transmission went dead, and all five planes were simply gone.

Where did the planes and their crews disappear to? One investigator said they had "vanished as completely as if they had flown to Mars."

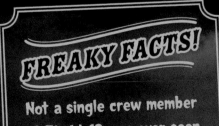

FREAKY FACTS!

Not a single crew member of Flight 19 was ever seen again, and no hints of the wreckages have ever been found. Official navy records say the planes went down "for reasons unknown."

CREW OF FLIGHT 19

OCEAN GRAVEYARDS

Whether they go down for paranormal reasons or just mechanical failure, the ocean floor is littered with the wreckages of sunken ships and downed planes. One of the biggest ocean "graveyards" is in Truk Lagoon, a region in the Pacific Ocean near New Guinea. The site has more than 40 Japanese ships and 250 aircraft that were lost to the sea during World War II. But not just that—divers can also see sunken tanks, trucks, and a whole ecosystem of sea life that has taken over.

15

A huge search team was sent out to look for crew members and the wrecked planes of Flight 19, but nothing was ever found. Adding to the mystery—and tragedy—of Flight 19 is a PBM Mariner, a rescue plane sent to look for the five missing planes. The plane vanished while flying over the Bermuda Triangle in an aerial search for any sign of Flight 19. A ship in the area later reported seeing a "huge fireball" in the area around the time the PBM Mariner would have been there, but nobody knows for sure if this fireball had anything to do with the rescue plane.

The disappearance of Flight 19 and the PBM Mariner are often pointed to as the starting point for the legend of the Bermuda Triangle's paranormal power. Would you want to take a trip through the Bermuda Triangle?

FREAKY FACTS!

The Bermuda Triangle is often home to waterspouts, which are whirling columns of air and water mist—in other words, a water tornado.

WATERSPOUT

16

WHAT'S THE DEAL WITH THE BERMUDA TRIANGLE?

Why have so many vessels and planes been lost in the area of the Bermuda Triangle? One problem is that the triangle is one of only two places on earth where compasses often can't work correctly. Inside the triangle, magnetic north (where your compass points) and true north (where the North Pole is) line up, which makes compass reading tricky. The area also has underwater trenches up to 27,500 feet (8,382 m) that could be hiding the vanished crafts.

THE EXACT AREA OF THE BERMUDA TRIANGLE HAS BEEN DEBATED, BUT MOST PEOPLE AGREE THAT IF IT EXISTS, IT'S FOUND BETWEEN BERMUDA, FLORIDA, AND PUERTO RICO.

DÉJÀ VU

Have you ever gone somewhere or done something for the first time and it feels familiar, as if you've been there or done it before? That's called "déjà vu," a French term for "already seen." Most people only experience déjà vu once in a while. But some people have been known to experience recurring déjà vu, which means it happens to them over and over again. They constantly remember places, people, and things that should be completely new to them.

Psychologists studying déjà vu think it has something to do with the way the human brain works—but other people think déjà vu is the result of special powers that allow people to see into alternate realities or even predict the future.

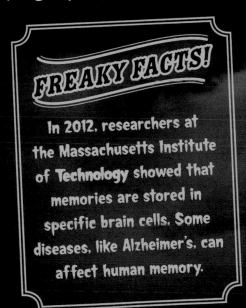

FREAKY FACTS!

In 2012, researchers at the Massachusetts Institute of Technology showed that memories are stored in specific brain cells. Some diseases, like Alzheimer's, can affect human memory.

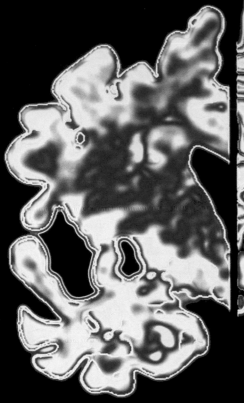

ALZHEIMER'S BRAIN

HEALTHY BRAIN

WHAT ARE MEMORIES?

Sometimes people who all experienced the same thing remember it very differently. This is because memories are made up of so many different elements that the brain has to work very hard to keep them all in order. When you remember a person, you might remember their name, their appearance, when and where you last saw them, how they smelled, what you talked about ... it's easy for the mind to get all those details mixed up!

Science says déjà vu is just a mix-up in the brain, but believers in the paranormal say it could be proof of parallel universes. In that theory, there are many universes besides our own, and they're all slightly different. When a person experiences déjà vu, what they're feeling is parallel universes lining up, so that the "you" in this universe and the "you" in another universe are experiencing the same thing at the same time.

So is déjà vu something that happens when you accidentally get a glimpse into another universe? Or is it just the brain struggling with a memory mix-up? So far, neither paranormal theorists nor scientists have been able to say for sure.

FREAKY FACTS!

Scientists say our universe is always expanding and has been ever since the Big Bang. The Big Bang is a scientific theory, or explanation, that suggests the beginning of the universe came from a huge explosion of matter.

BIG BANG

WE'VE LEARNED A LOT ABOUT SPACE SINCE THE FIRST MOON LANDING IN 1969, BUT THERE'S SO MUCH MORE ABOUT ITS FAR REACHES WE DON'T YET KNOW.

MULTIPLE UNIVERSES

Scientists and paranormal theorists alike have debated the existence of multiple universes—the multiverse—for many years. Some people even think there may be *infinite* universes with infinite **versions** of every person on Earth. So if you were struggling to decide what shirt you wanted to wear this morning, don't worry. If there really are infinite universes, a different version of you wore the shirt you didn't.

MYSTERIOUS OBJECTS

While examining the damage caused by a small fire on their property near Jacksonville, Florida, in 1974, the Betz family found a steel ball that was about 8 inches (20 cm) across, perfectly round, had no noticeable seams, and was plain except for a single triangle design. Things got really freaky when the Betz family brought the ball home. Soon, it began vibrating and making strange sounds. If someone pushed the orb away, it rolled right back. On sunny days, the ball was very active; on cloudy days, it laid low.

The Betzes sent the ball to the navy to be tested, and a marine spokesperson later admitted that they hadn't been able to figure out where the ball came from. All they could say was, "There's certainly something odd about it."

FREAKY FACTS!

When NASA's 78-ton (71 mt) Skylab space station fell from space in 1979, they were fined $400 for littering by the Shire of Esperance in Western Australia.

SOMEONE NOT FAMILIAR WITH THE RUSSIAN SPACE PROGRAM MIGHT HAVE THOUGHT GAGARIN'S SHIP WAS ACTUALLY AN ALIEN CRAFT!

VOSTOK 1 CONTROL PANEL

"ARE YOU FROM OUTER SPACE?"

The first human to ever visit space was a Russian named Yuri Gagarin. His spacecraft, the *Vostok 1*, launched into space on April 12, 1961, and returned the same day after 108 minutes of space travel. When Gagarin landed in a field, a family that lived nearby greeted him. When they asked jokingly whether he could have come from space, Gagarin said, "As a matter of fact, I have!"

WHAT HAPPENED AT ROSWELL?

On July 7, 1947, something fell from the sky and crashed on a ranch near Roswell, New Mexico. Newspapers reported it was a flying saucer, but the government soon claimed it was a weather balloon. As time went by, some wondered whether that story wasn't a cover for something more, well, paranormal.

Years later, retired US Army lieutenant colonel Philip J. Corso published a book called *The Day After Roswell* that claimed the weather balloon story was just that: a story. Corso said he was part of a secret government program that studied alien technology discovered in the Roswell crash and used it to invent things like the computer chip. Corso also claims he saw "a four-foot human-shaped figure with arms … four-fingered hands, and an oversized … lightbulb-shaped head."

FREAKY FACTS!

Extraterrestrial life probably won't be the little green men of the movies. Many scientists are simply looking for bacteria and microorganisms. But one professor at Cambridge University thinks aliens might look just like us!

A UFO, OR UNIDENTIFIED FLYING OBJECT, IS WHAT PEOPLE CALL SUPPOSED ALIEN SPACESHIPS. THE EVENT NEAR ROSWELL, NEW MEXICO, IN 1947 IS PROBABLY THE MOST FAMOUS UFO SIGHTING.

1952 UFO SIGHTING IN PASSAIC, NEW JERSEY

ROCK THAT'S SAID TO HAVE BEEN SPLIT IN TWO BY A SPACESHIP IMPACT NEAR ROSWELL, NEW MEXICO

WE COME IN PEACE

Most alien movies show aliens coming to Earth, but it may be that if humans ever make contact with an alien species, we'll be the ones saying, "We come in peace!" NASA is constantly searching the universe for planets with intelligent life. In a galaxy of at least 100 billion planets, many NASA researchers find it easy to believe there's life on other planets. Some people even think humans will meet extraterrestrial life within 20 years!

25

THE GURDON LIGHT

The year was 1931, and Louis McBride was angry that William McClain wouldn't give him more hours of work on the railroad. According to legend, McBride killed McClain, and the Gurdon Light is McClain's ghostly lantern glowing. Other legends say the Gurdon Light comes from the lantern of another railroad worker who is searching for his head, which he lost when he fell in the path of a train.

The light, named for Gurdon, Arkansas, is often described as "bobbing around," like a lantern swinging. Witnesses have said the light moves away when you try to approach it. Attempts to explain away the light as a reflection of headlights have been dismissed, as the light has shown up in local history since long before the nearby interstate was built.

FREAKY FACTS!

William McClain's lantern is far from the first reported ghost light. Such phenomena are common in local legends. In fact, they even have a special name: will-o'-the-wisps.

WILL-O'-THE-WHAT?

Back in the old days, a will-o'-the-wisp was thought to be the light from a fairy or spirit that would lead travelers deep into bogs and forests, most often to their death. Stories and legends about will-o'-the-wisps are found all over the world. In Brazil, they're called *boitatá*, in Japan *onibi*, and in Scotland, they're called a *spunkie*. Some will-o'-the-wisps are thought to be caused by combustion of natural gases.

YOU MIGHT BE FAMILIAR WITH ANOTHER NAME FOR WILL-O'-THE-WISPS: JACK-O'-LANTERNS!

MOTHMAN

The first sighting of the Mothman was in Point Pleasant, West Virginia, in 1966. Gravediggers reported seeing a man-sized, flying creature glide over them. They described it as a "huge, birdlike creature with eyes like red reflectors and a wingspan of 10 feet." The same night, 100 miles (161 km) north, a contractor spotted the creature in a field near his house right before his TV went haywire and his dog, Bandit, began howling. Bandit chased the creature into the field and never returned.

A month later, two couples spotted the creature following their car. They described it as "a flying man with 10-foot wings." So what was it? Some people think it was just a large bird, like a crane. Others believe it was an alien or other supernatural being.

FREAKY FACTS!

Not including the Mothman, moths can get pretty big. The Atlas moth's wingspan covers an area as large as 62 square inches (400 sq cm)! At the other end of the range, a tiny moth from Africa is just .04 inch (1 mm) long.

COLLAPSE OF THE SILVER BRIDGE

The Silver Bridge Disaster on December 15, 1967, was one of the worst tragedies Point Pleasant had ever seen. Forty-six lives were lost when a piece of the bridge broke, causing the whole thing to collapse. John Keel, a journalist and author, suggested in his book *The Mothman Prophecies* that the tragedy was linked to the sightings of the Mothman. Though most experts have dismissed this theory, the idea lives on in the Mothman legend.

GLOSSARY

archaeological: having to do with the study of human history and prehistory through the excavation of sites and the analysis of artifacts and other physical remains

artifact: something made by humans in the past

assassinate: to kill someone, especially a public figure

audible: something heard or able to be heard

insomnia: the inability to fall or remain asleep

medieval: relating to European history between about the years 500 and 1500

microorganism: a living thing so small it can only be seen using a microscope

phenomena: facts or events that are observed. The singular form is "phenomenon."

pseudoscience: a collection of beliefs or practices mistakenly regarded as being based on scientific method

psychologist: someone who studies the human mind and human behavior

technology: the way people do something using tools and the tools that they use

version: a certain form or type of something

FOR MORE INFORMATION

BOOKS

Allen, Judy. *Unexplained: An Encyclopedia of Curious Phenomena, Strange Superstitions, and Ancient Mysteries.* Boston, MA: Kingfisher, 2006.

Gibson, Marley, Patrick Burns, and Dave Schrader. *The Other Side: A Teen's Guide to Ghost Hunting and the Paranormal.* Boston, MA: Houghton Mifflin Harcourt, 2009.

Nelson, Kristen. *Investigating Hypnosis and Trances.* New York, NY: Britannica Educational Publishing, 2016.

WEBSITES

Five Legendary Lost Cities That Have Never Been Found
ancient-origins.net/unexplained-phenomena/five-legendary-lost-cities-have-never-been-found-004407
Read about five cities that show up repeatedly in legends, but have never been found.

Unexplained Phenomena
science.howstuffworks.com/science-vs-myth/unexplained-phenomena
Read more about unexplained phenomena across the globe.

INDEX